KINDERGARTEN NUMBER FUN

Fun-filled Activities

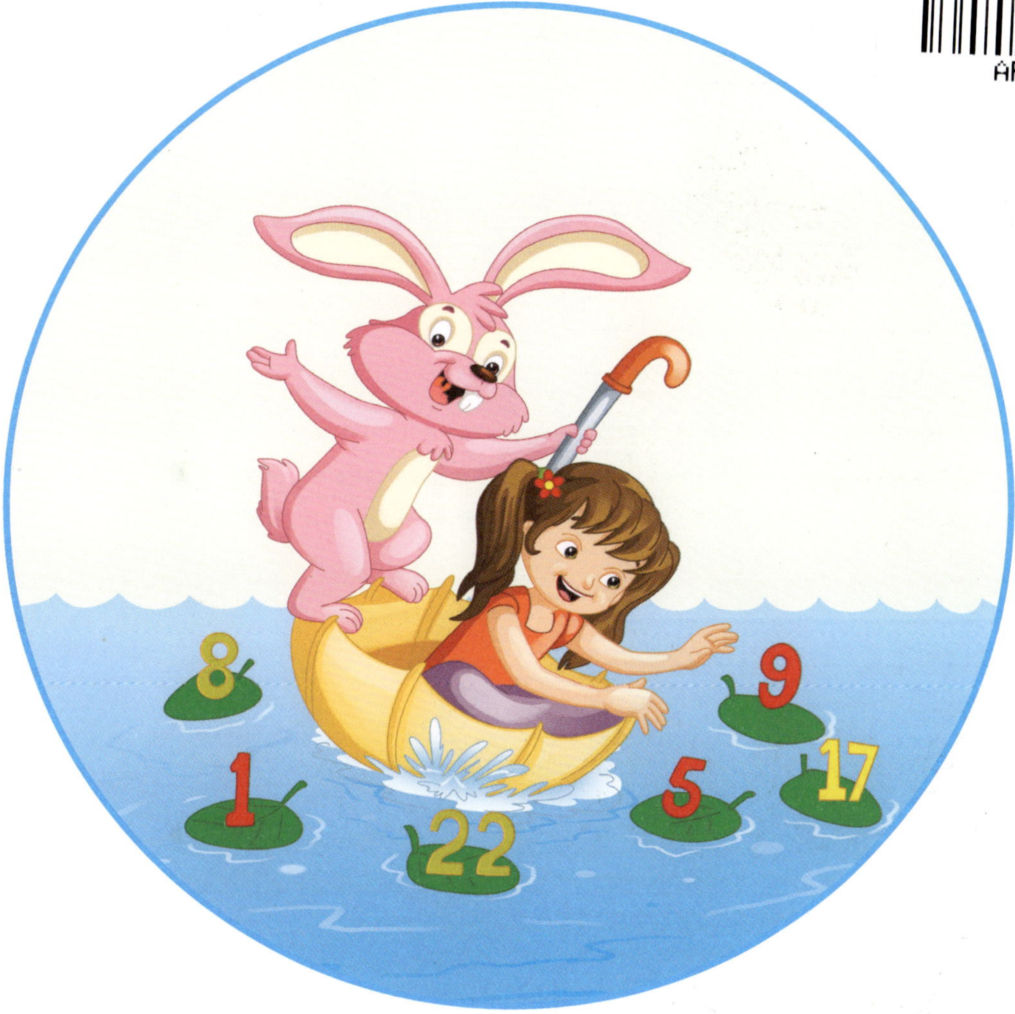

Om KIDZ
An imprint of Om Books International

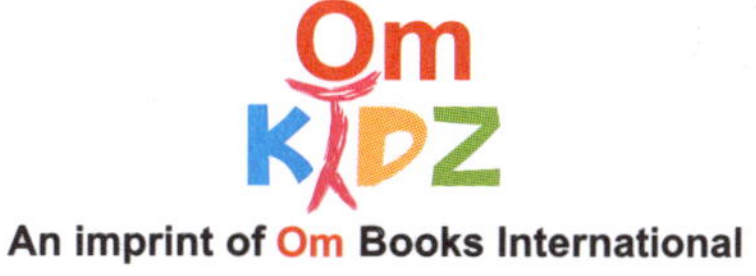

Write Numbers 0-5

Write numbers for these words.

zero

one

two

three

four

five

Count And Match

Count the objects in each box. Draw a line from the box to the correct number.

0

1

2

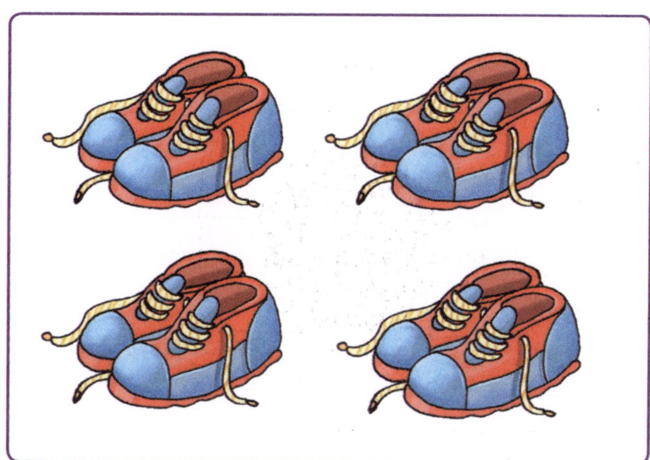

3

4

5

Count And Write

Count the animals and write the number.

Write Numbers 6-10

Count the pictures in each box. Write the number and number word.

Count And Circle

How many are there in each group? Draw a circle (O) around the correct number.

6 5 8

4 7 9

8 5 6

7 10 3

6 7 9

Count And Write

How many are there in each group? Write the number.

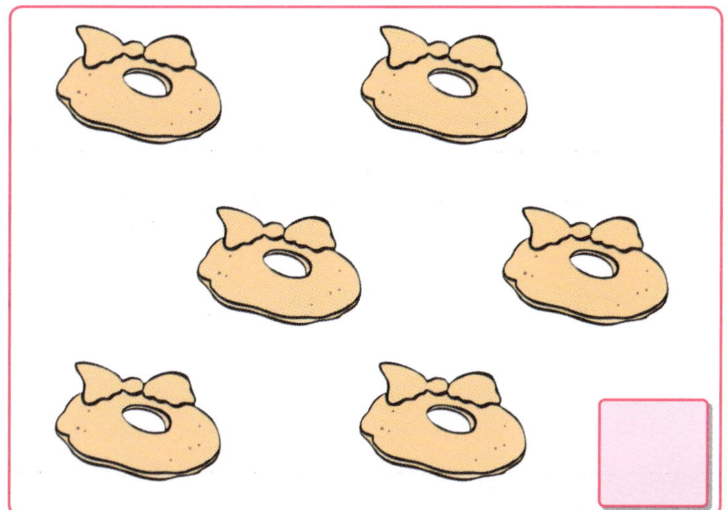

Let's Draw

Read the number.

Draw that many shapes. One in each box has been drawn for you.

9

7

10

8

6

Numerical Order

Connect the stars from 0-10. Colour the picture.

Where Are The Numbers?

Find numbers 0-9 in the picture. Circle (O) them.

Write Numbers 11-15

Write numbers for these words.

eleven

twelve

thirteen

fourteen

fifteen

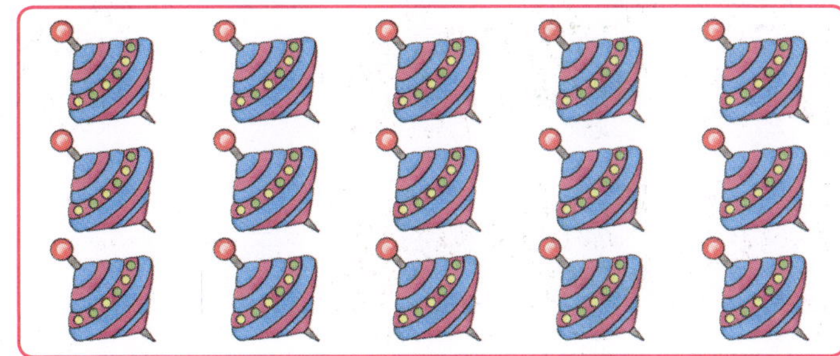

Count And Write

How many are there in each group? Count and write.

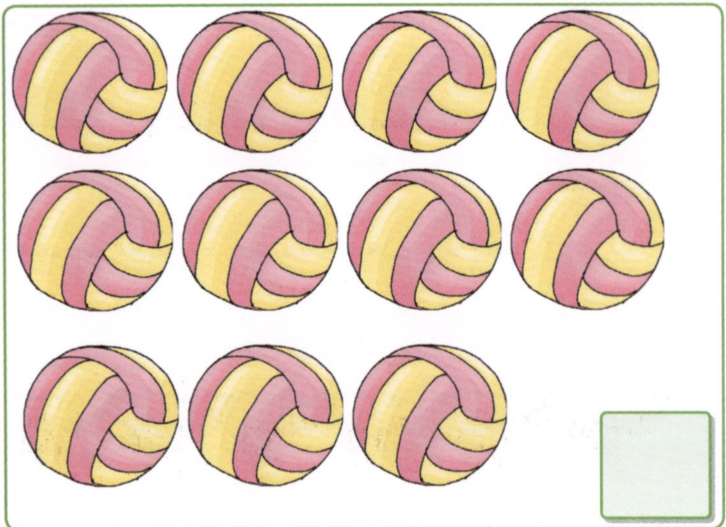

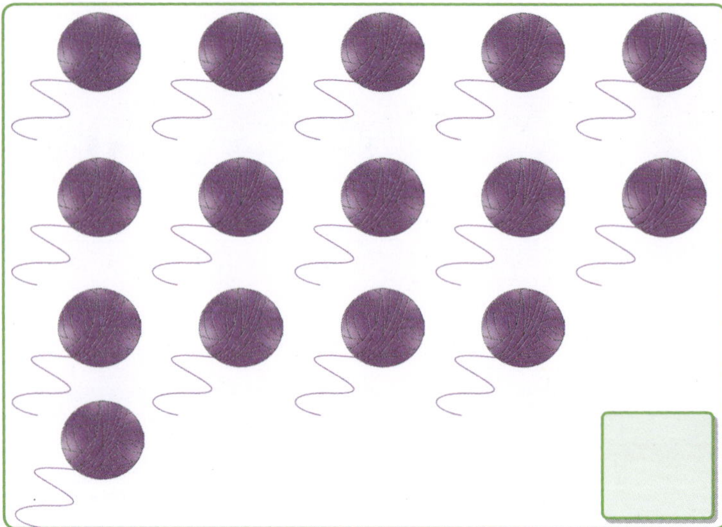

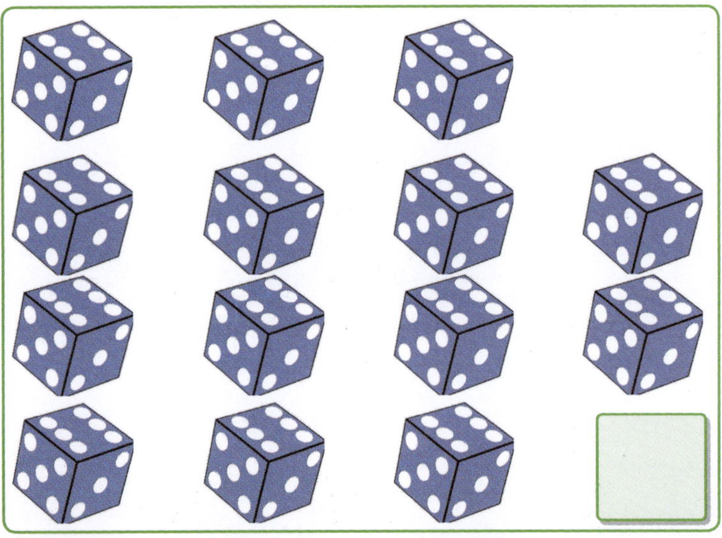

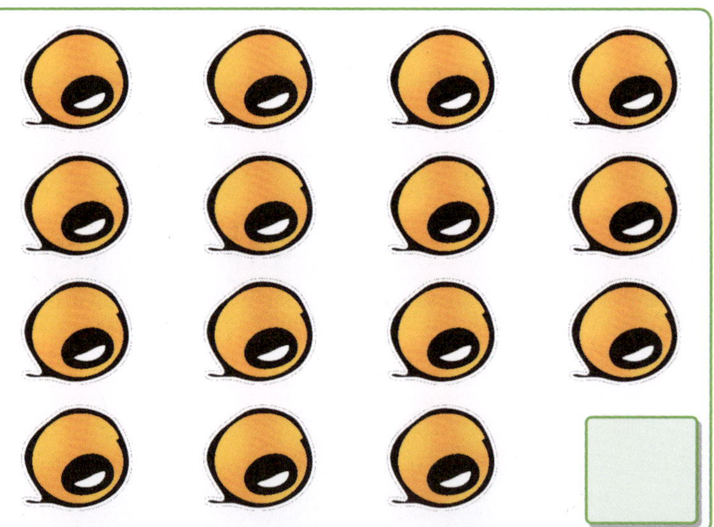

Writing Numbers 16-20

Write number words for these numbers.

16 ______________

17 ______________

18 ______________

19 ______________

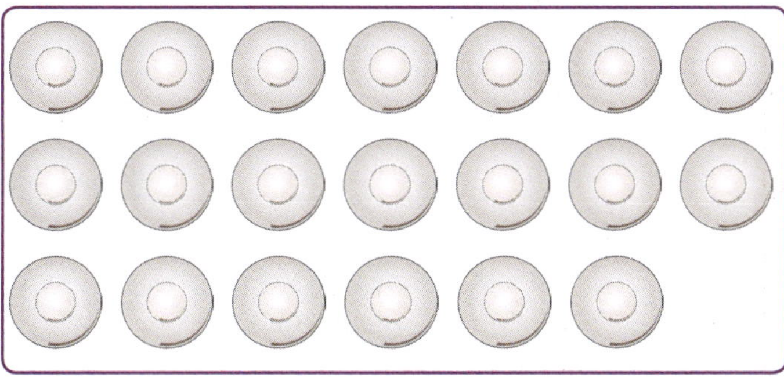

20 ______________

Count And Match

How many are there in each group? Draw a line from the group to the correct number.

20

18

16

17

19

Count Backwards

Draw pathways by counting backwards. Write the missing numbers.

What Comes Before?

8 comes **before 9**

Which number comes **before** these numbers? Write them.

____ 12 13	____ 6 7
____ 15 16	____ 13 14
____ 19 20	____ 5 6

What Comes In Between?

12 comes **between 11** and **13**

Write the number that comes in **between** these numbers.

14	______	16
8	______	10
18	______	20
13	______	15
16	______	18
7	______	9

What Comes After?

15 comes **after 14**

Which number comes **after** these numbers? Write them.

12 13 ____	10 11 ____
8 9 ____	5 6 ____
14 15 ____	17 18 ____

Same Number

How many bunnies are there?

4 3 6

How many carrots are there?

5 4 3

The number of bunnies is the same as the number of carrots.

Circle **YES** if the groups show **same** number of objects and **NO** if they don't.

YES

NO

Same Number

Draw fruits in the empty baskets to match the same number of fruits in the filled baskets.

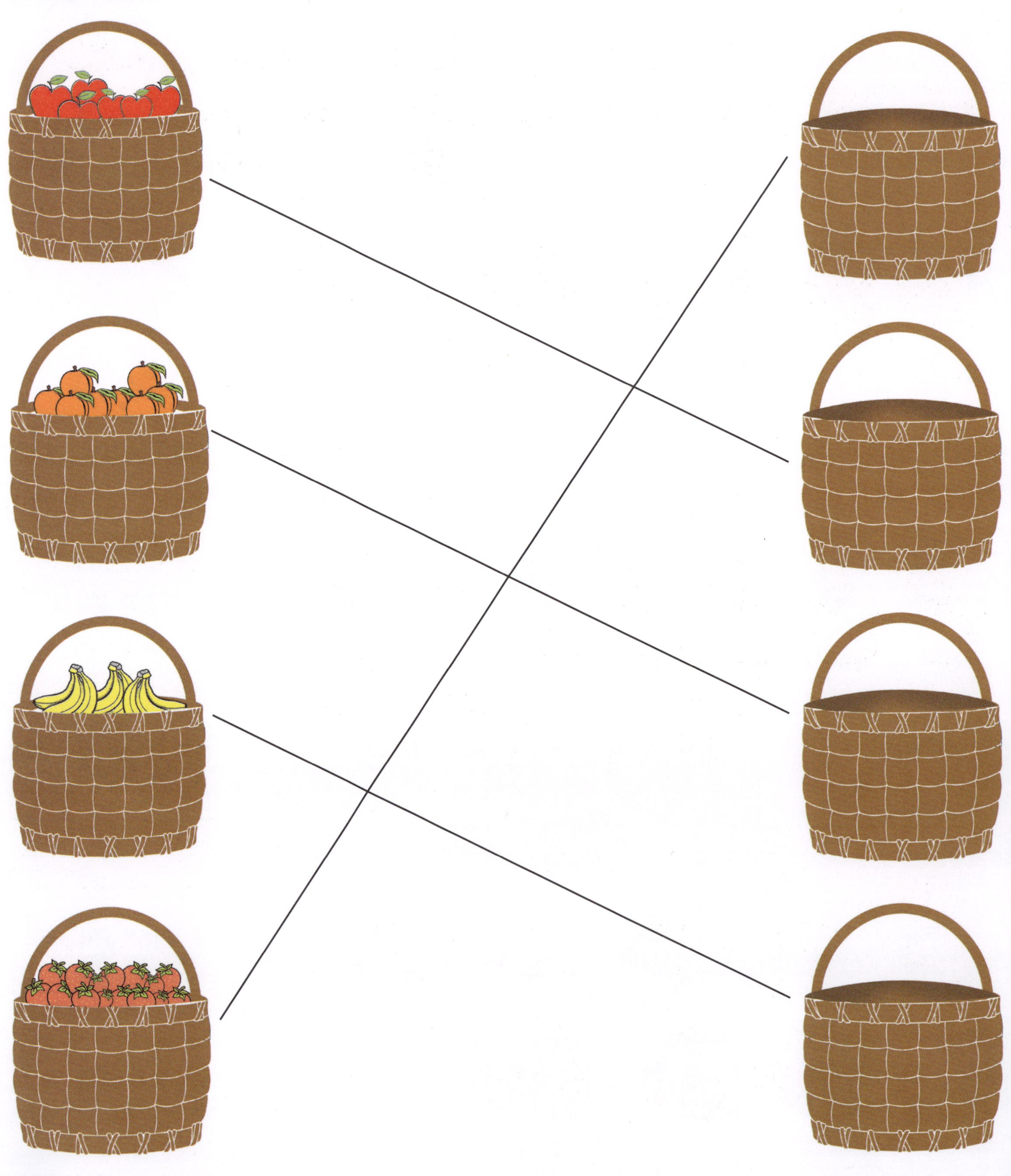

Which Number Is Less?

Match one-to-one to identify the group with fewer objects.

Tick (✓) the number that is less.

Which Group Has Fewer?

Count the number of objects in each group and write the number.

Circle (O) the group that has **fewer** objects.

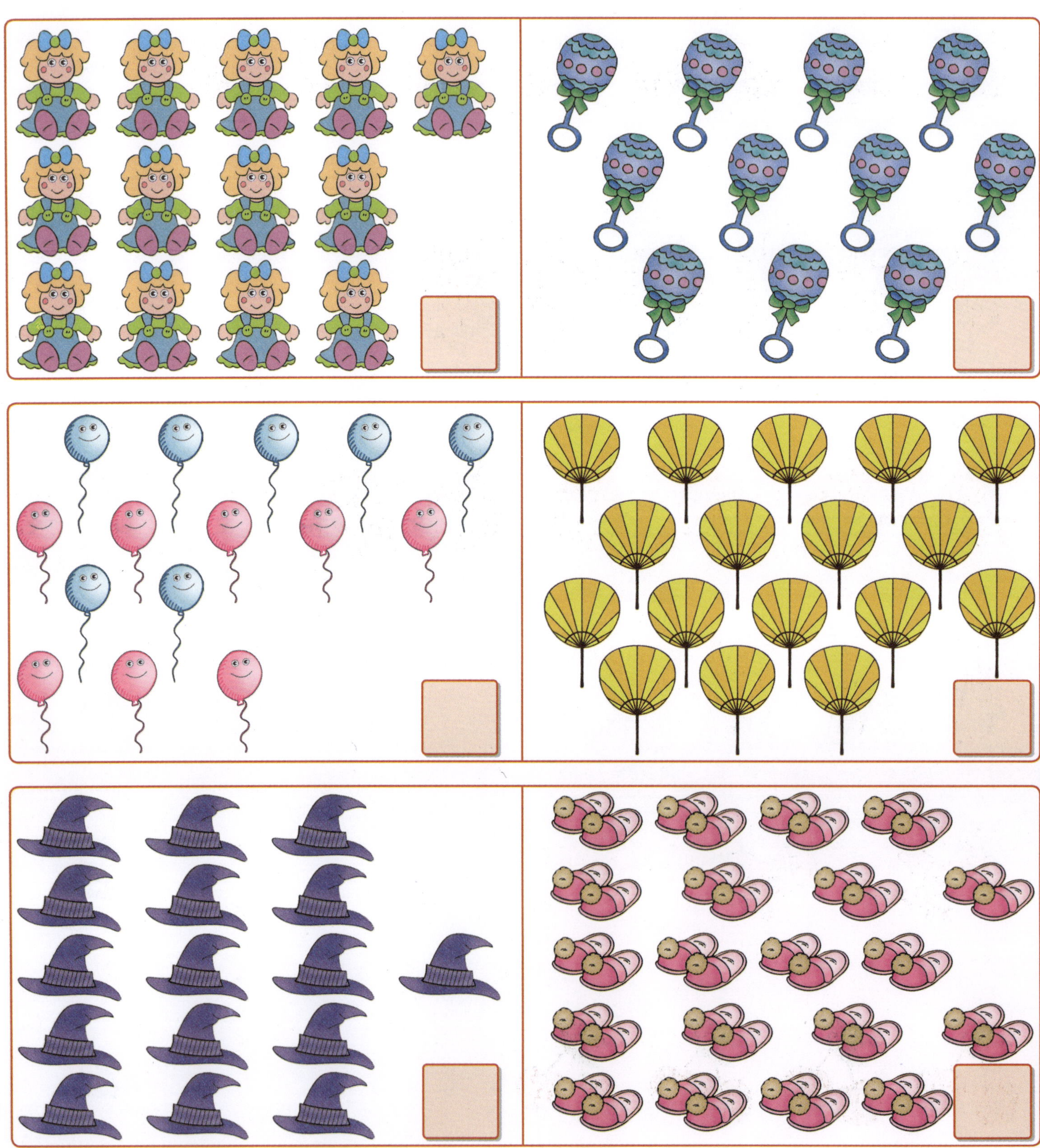

Which Number Is Less?

Read the number and draw that many ⬭s.

Circle (O) the number that is less.

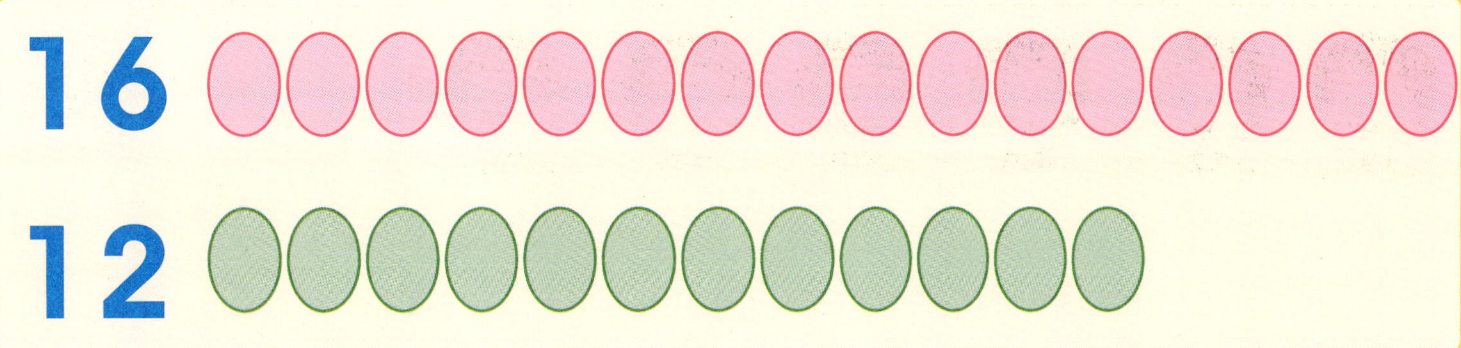

10

13

8

6

15

13

Which Number Is Greater?

Match one-to-one to identify the group with **more** objects.

Tick (✓) the number that is **greater**.

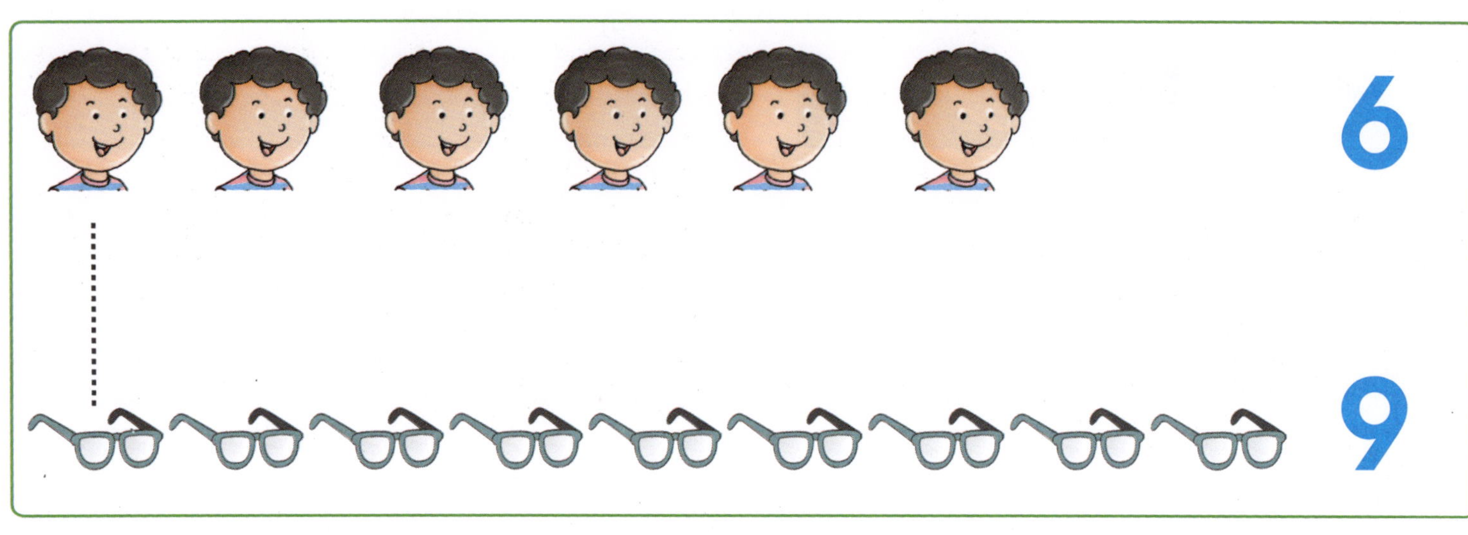

Which Group Has More?

Count the number of objects in each group and write the number.

Circle (O) the group that has more objects.

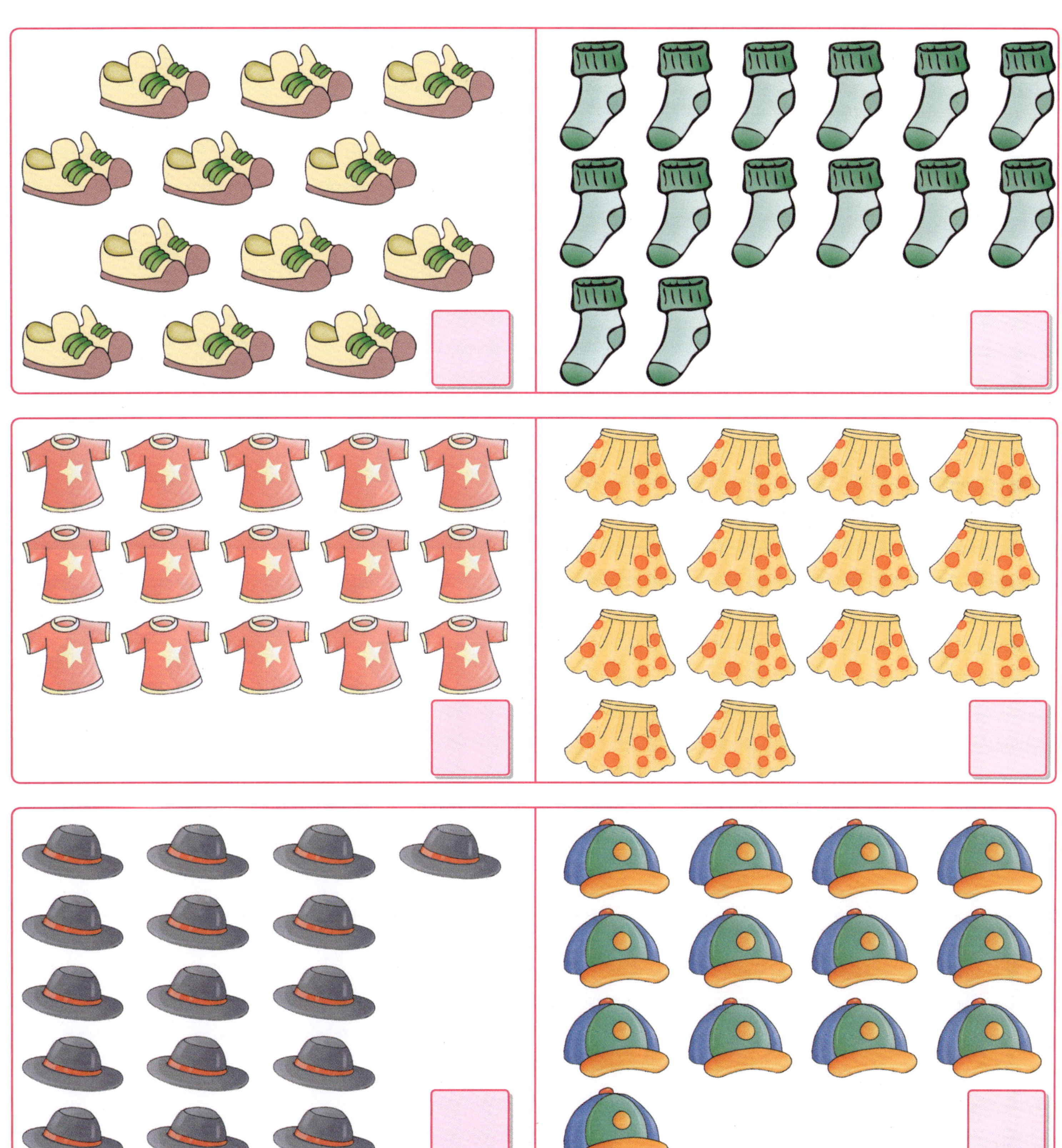

Which Number Is Greater?

Read the number and draw that many ☆s.

Circle (O) the number that is greater.

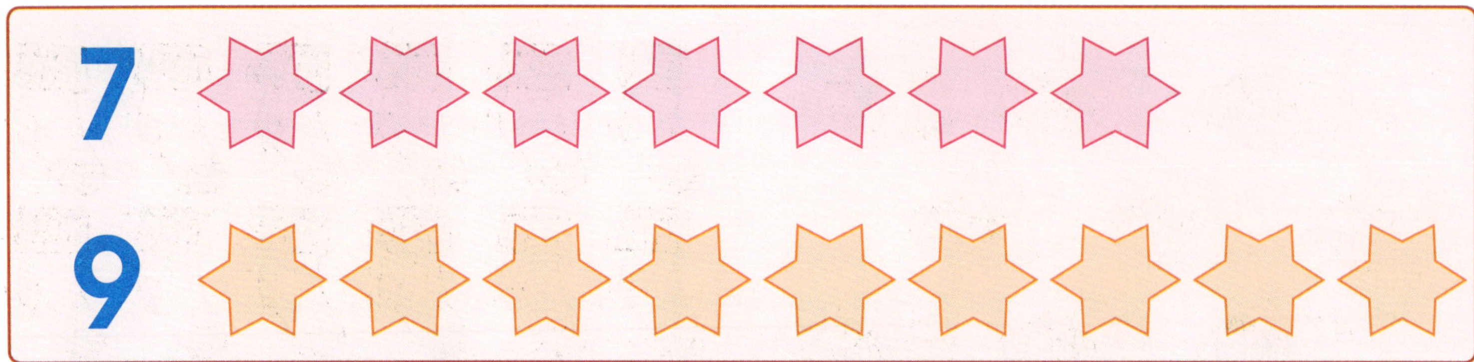

12

11

14

16

13

10

Writing Numbers As Tallies

This is how we write numbers as tally marks.

1	|	6	𝍸 |
2	||	7	𝍸 ||
3	|||	8	𝍸 |||
4	||||	9	𝍸 ||||
5	𝍸	10	𝍸 𝍸

Draw a line from the number to its tally mark.

10	||||
6	𝍸 |||
4	𝍸
8	𝍸 |
5	𝍸 𝍸

Writing Numbers As Tallies

Draw tally marks to show the numbers.

Join The Dots

Connect the dots from 1-20. Colour the picture.

Answer Key

Page 2
zero 0
one 1
two 2
three 3
four 4
five 5
Page 3
0
1
2
3
4
5
Page 4
3
4
0
5
2
1
Page 5
6 six
7 seven
8 eight
9 nine
10 ten
Page 6
6 5 8
4 7 9
8 5 6
7 10 3
6 7 9
Page 7
10
8
6
7
9
9
Page 8
9
7
10
8
6
Page 9
0
1
2
3
4
5
6
7
8
9
10
Page 10

Answer Key

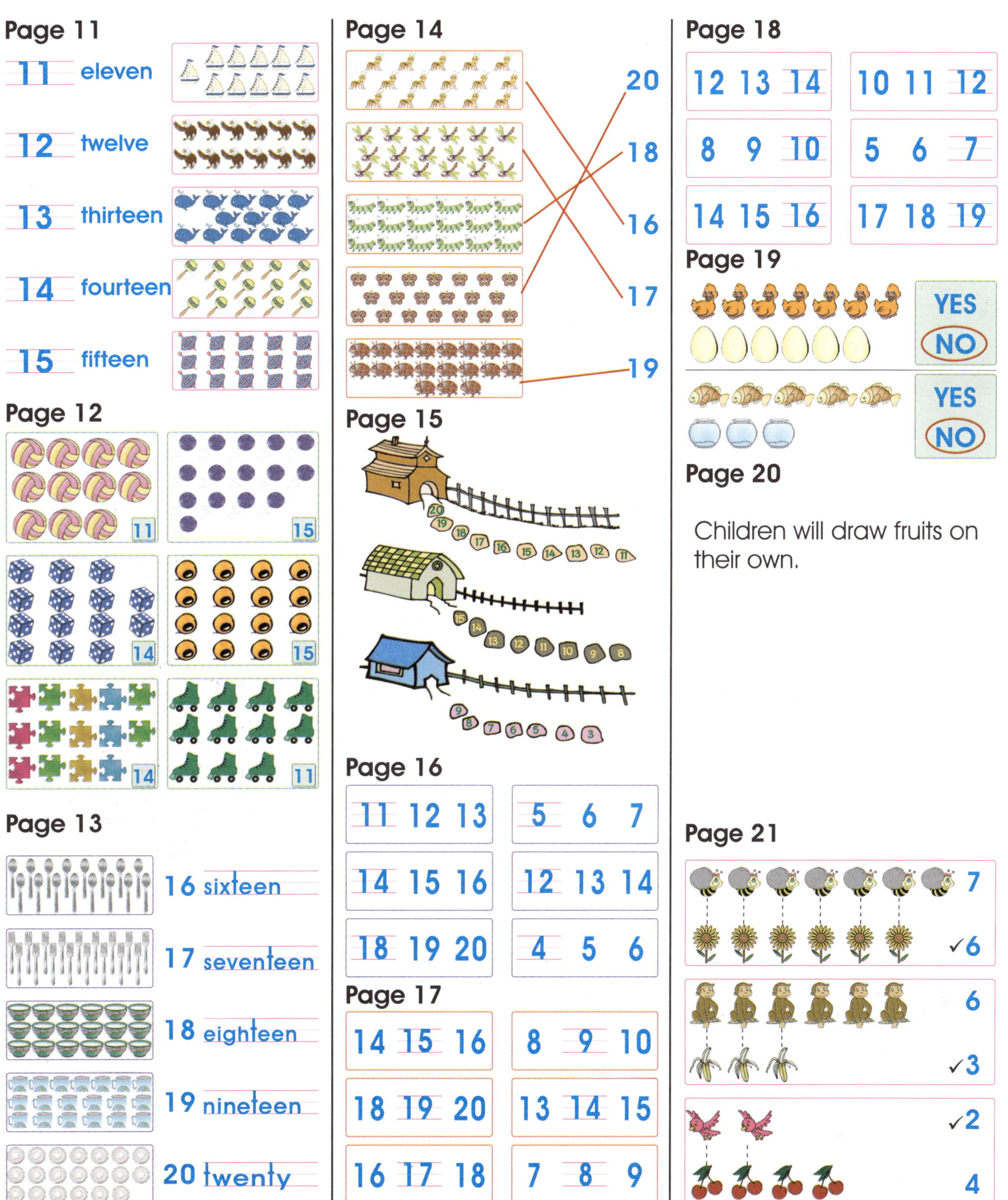

Page 11
11 eleven
12 twelve
13 thirteen
14 fourteen
15 fifteen
Page 12
11
15
14
15
14
11
Page 13
16 sixteen
17 seventeen
18 eighteen
19 nineteen
20 twenty
Page 14
20
18
16
17
19
Page 15
20 19 18 17 16 15 14 13 12 11
15 14 13 12 11 10 9 8
9 8 7 6 5 4 3
Page 16
11 12 13
5 6 7
14 15 16
12 13 14
18 19 20
4 5 6
Page 17
14 15 16
8 9 10
18 19 20
13 14 15
16 17 18
7 8 9
Page 18
12 13 14
10 11 12
8 9 10
5 6 7
14 15 16
17 18 19
Page 19
YES
NO
YES
NO
Page 20
Children will draw fruits on their own.
Page 21
7
✓6
6
✓3
✓2
4

Answer Key

Page 22

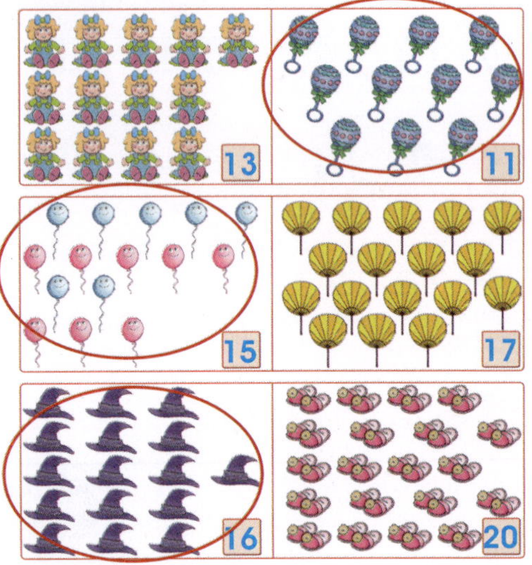

Page 23

16
12

10
13

8
6

15
13

Page 24

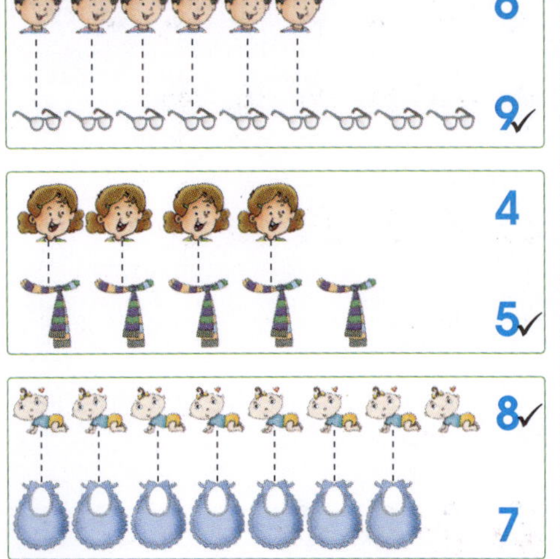

Page 25

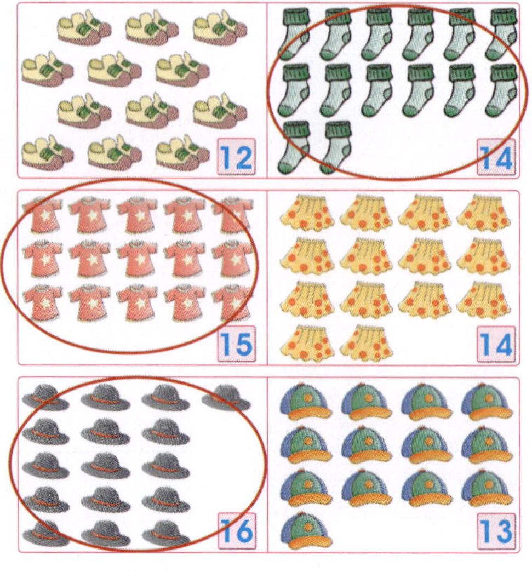

Page 26

14
16

13
10

Page 27

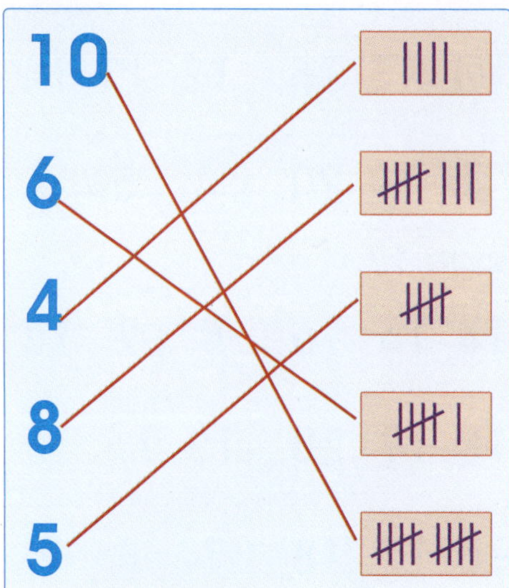

Page 28

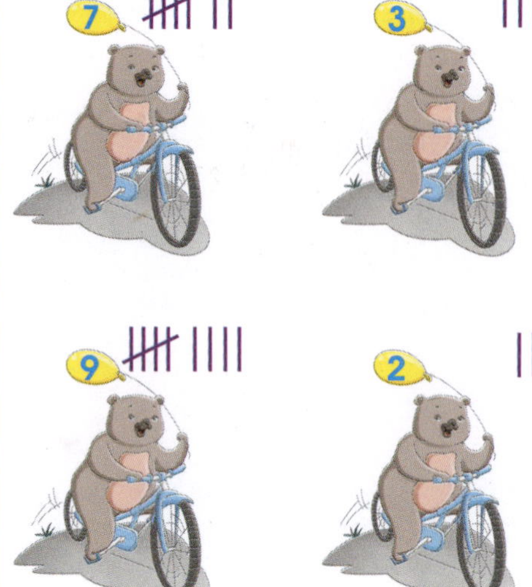

Page 29